The contents and creations herein are the property of their respective artist(s) and may not be used or reproduced without explicit written consent. The following works have been donated from prisoners across the United States and are published with permission in order to amplify the voices of queer and trans people surviving imprisonment.

A.B.O. Comix Collective is sustained by volunteers, community donations, grant funding, and various daring bank heists. We run on the perserverance, bravery, kindness, empathy, and love that our contributors share with us.

Edited by Ollie Mills
Transcribed by Cass & Casper Cendre
Cover Design by Laura Lutrell

Table of Contents

A Queer Prisoner's Poetry Anthology, Vol. 2

About

A.B.O. Comix is a collective of creators and activists who work to amplify the voices of LGBTQ prisoners through art. By working closely with prison abolitionist and queer advocacy organizations, we aim to keep queer prisoners connected to outside community and help them in the fight toward liberation. The profits we generate go back to incarcerated artists, especially those with little to no resources. Using the DIY ideology of "punk-zine" culture, A.B.O. Comix was formed with the philosophy of mutual support, community, and friendship.

Our collective is working towards compassionate accountability without relying on the state or its sycophants. A.B.O. Comix believes our interpersonal and societal issues can be solved without locking people in cages. Our mission is to combat the culture that treats humans as disposable and disproportionately criminalizes the most marginalized amongst us. Through artistic activism, we hope to proliferate the idea that a better world means redefining our concepts of justice.

Find us online at www.abocomix.com and @a.b.o.comix on Instagram

With love and solidarity, A.B.O. Comix Collective

Foreword

No pretense
Only postage, time & authority's whim

No biopsy
Nor cautious stripping
Only breath before the shock

Loss of consciousness sublimated
Into art, pride & joy

I have been rescued by these poems.

I think about the fever of writing -
That urgency, that heat,
That feeling beyond feeling

We are creating an antidote to detachment
Bathing in the courage to touch despair and
spring back; keep on.

Engaging glancingly with our most
painful, real, realities -
the potential of
what we write
is unknown
to us.

We write to
plant seeds
in each other's mouths

And menace the world together
with no distance.

- Ollie Mills

Part 1

i declare peace for myself

Mocha Scroggins | Ain't I a Woman

Today I woke up and looked in the
mirror, and asked myself:
Ain't I a Woman?

With long hair that I pull over my
face when stressed?
Okay after, just knowing that I'm blessed?
My beautiful eyes that I wink with a
smile, come when I swish my hips.
Unconsciously aware of all the
stares that come when I dip my hips.
Into a nice slow rhythm, that I know will
attract.
Attention for my beautiful black soul,
that shows my culture's intact.
Ain't I a Woman?

Who comes from the lions of all those
women before me.
Who understands the pressures and pains
that would be associated with these
beautifully-crafted legs of a gazelle
that are Mocha-coated and built to excel.

Don't you see the dreams in the eyes
of this spectacular creature?
How she steps around the traps that
predators have set for her?
Oh, what a sight it is, but still so sad.
That in this day and age she still
has to ask:
Ain't I a Woman?

Chris Lafamilia | Knowledge

They tried to act like we don't know
Gadafee
Or wasn't gone take off like a car full of
nitris
See we were born righteous
Stripped of all our knowledge
And made to praise new gods
Our grands couldn't write but when
They find us the results gone be astouding
Cold as the Caucasus Mountains
Where Caucasians were founde
Then they came down south threw us off
like they mounded
Blessed every month threw us 28 like some
ounces
Said let's talk about it, emphasized like
we was counseling
Now we reciprocate hate
Kick it out like a bouncer
What you expect? Nothing less than
repatriate the founders
We were kings and queens when the mf'ers
found us
But we were never equal as people
I'm no accountant but the death rate is
countless
Steady screaming #BlackLivesMatter - but
do they count us? If you rap or ball they
make exceptions profoundly
This is a message to anyone who needs to
hear it:
When your hands are tied the deepest
spirit will make them feel it: respect
yourself

8

Stay true, spread knowledge to your
children
The more we know, the more we grow and
minimize the killings!

So power to the people so the people
never live in fear
Damn it ain't no Justice here
Ain't nothing Changed
They still gone treat us like we're off
the ship
And then take ownership
Like we ain't never owned our shit!

Trouble the Goat | Untitled

As I close my eyes and search my soul
In hopes of covering each & every base,
Like racism & rapist & my thoughts on
inauguration
I'm impatient! Because, well I'm hungry
but these niggas is always hatin'
& by "niggas" I mean black brothas & black
sistahs
Of our nation.
So why claim 'em?
Bring back the segregation!
& then maybe we'll remember what it took
To be a nation.

'Cause see:
We don't stick together anyway!
We won't turn up with what's needed
We won't turn up on the enemies
We won't prove that we're united, black
lives matter nothin' anyways!
We won't lead by an example when it's
needed in so many ways

I'm baffled!

The contradictions of the system -
Rehabilitating who?
More like punishing some children
Telling grown fucks what to do,
Ain't no way to gain victory
I'm so sick of being fooled.
Ain't no reason in black history
That's blasphemy!
'Cause we're still victims of embezzlement

40 acres & a mule? Man miss me with that
craziness - that's ludacris!
When we own more than just a little bit
I'm sick of it!
The way they play on our intelligence
I'm sick of it!
The contributions to conspiracy!

White man kill a nigga
& he gets set free

Nigga kill a nigga
& it's 15

Nigga kill a white man?
That's life!

The truth hurts, but a lie won't
Make it right!

Mocha Scroggins | The Face of Emmett Till

Face the Face of Emmett Till
'til justice finds him whole.
Face the wounds that haunt us still,
still restless in his soul.
The ballooned orbs where cheeks should be,
the bludgeoned smile that we can't see.
Look upon the gruesome marks
of Jim Crow's heavy toll.

Peer into the casket, gasp at
evil's wicked hands.
Peer into the past
unmasked inhumanity of man.
The mangled form that was a boy.
The equal rights they can't destroy,
Look upon the Face that caused
the world to take a stand.

His mother bade us to look,
just look and let the whole world see.
She showed us what they took,
they showed their insecurity.
The stolen youth based on a lie,
the Face of Truth that cannot die.

Look upon the Face of one
who's finally been set free.
Embrace him in his loneliness,
he who died a martyr's death.
Embrace his endless liveliness,
for we are now his breath.
The struggle that has yet to be won.
The victory we must give her son.

The struggle that has yet to be won.
The victory we must give her son.
Look upon the Face
                    of all the work
                    that we have left.

KRAZYBWOY | The Storm

Like an crow in the blue sky
    another day flies by,
The storm is coming and where we go
    one, we go all.
Each panther has its own story that
    didn't end with them because
Once the storm blows it in our ears
    We will tell it time and again.
The storm is coming and where we go
    one, we go all.
Seeing the pain in the panthers' families,
    faces completely put into
Perspective. Why these lions fight
    with these panthers?
So these panthers do not and did not
    die in vain.
We honor and remember them as we
    call out each and
Every one of their names with a
    21 gun salute.

Shyra Bryant | Untitled

Racing thoughts like thunder inside the
stillness of a tiny cubicle.

Panicking like a racehorse, traveling the
ultimate distance.

Within one's mind, space seems clear as
day as memories fade.

Through temporary clouds, soaring with
eagles, feeling the rage of wild beasts.

Escaping body into spirit (for maybe a
second, it seems) possible movements
forsaken, vacant.

To excel is inhaling hope's exsistence,
letting not a chamber keep thee confined
mentally, or defined into judgement's
statistics, nor political views of
faceless expressions. Melting color with
burning gas, I tear at reflections of en-
slavement in glass-made doors.

I see addictions, diseases (also beauty)
within thee struggle to survive,
avoiding attachments one physically can't
grasp onto or emotionally let go.

Abandoning self-creations, neglecting
one's desires, satisfactions, cravings,
love. Leaving one starved and physically
drained, but mentally powerful beyond any
measure.

ashes of love and struggle
Panicking
like a racehorse.
Traveling the ultimate distance
with one's mind.

Power lies not in thee, steel metal,
keeping us intact and unmoved.

It exists in the stillness, the infinite.

Exploring endless bounds
and unlimited places to travel.

Even inside captivity,
spirit will not be contained.

Ms Jazzie Ferrari | My Center Peace

The outer world does not touch me.
I am in charge of my own being.
I guard my inner world
for it is there that I create.
I do whatever I need to do
to keep my inner world peaceful.

My inner peace is essential
for my health and well-being.
I go within and find that space
where all is quiet and serene.

I may see it
as a peaceful, deep, quiet pool
surrounded by green grass and tall,
silent trees.
I may feel it
as white, willowy clouds
upon which to lie and be caressed.
I may hear delightful music
that soothes my senses.

No matter how I choose
to experience my inner peace,
I find peace at this center of peace.

I am
I am the pureness
and stillness of the center of my
creative process.

The peace I create.
In peace I live
and move and experience life.

ashes of love and struggle

Because I keep myself centered in inner
peace, I have peace in my outer world.

Although others may have discord and
chaos, it does not touch me,
for I declare peace for myself.

I'm a very,
very beautiful black, strong, trans woman
and proud of that.

Although there may be madness all around
me, I am calm and peaceful.

The universe is one of great order
and peacefulness,
and I reflect this in my everyday life.

The stars and the planets
do not need to be worried or fearful in
order to maintain their heavenly
orbits.

Nor does chaotic thinking contribute to my
peaceful existence in
Life.

I choose to express peacefulness
for
I am
peace.

Mocha Scroggins | American and Trans

This is supposed to be the home
of the brave and land of the free.
The land of the free is debatable
as far as I can see.
Why are some people judged
and ridiculed for what they are?
Wanting to be treated as a person
shouldn't have to be wished upon a star.

Don't get me wrong, times have changed
and we have come a long way.
But the way things are is not the
way things should stay.
Nobody should be made to feel different
or that they are less than.
We need more love and acceptance
and less hate than there has ever been.

No youth should be made to feel
that there is no way out.
Taking their own life should never
enter their minds or come about.
Being bullied for being different is
something nobody should have to tolerate.
Hate is something that is taught.
People are not born in that mental state.

Like every other person, trans
people have feelings and a heartbeat
To all the holy people that say:
"it's an abomination, it's wrong."
Please, have a seat.
Not to judge and love thy neighbor,
in the Bible it does say.

ashes of love and struggle

Treating others how you want to be treated
is the right way.

What if something you did or said
was responsible for ending a life?

Some people have been damaged,
over and over with a cut of a knife.

Something as simple as being kind to
someone could get them through another
day.

Maybe one day, people will feel free
and safe to live as American and trans...

A Queer Prisoner's Poetry Anthology, Vol. 2

Part 2

*we are held
accountable to
the abstraction
of justice*

David Snyder | Diego Dueñas

#2255506
used to have
     a number

used to be
     son
     brother

the sanctity of life
     obliterated
     desecrated

anonymous
     death

most oblivious
     mired in the mundane
     indifferent to His suffering

ashes of love and struggle
we are held accountable
          to the abstraction
                              of
                 justice

prison industrial complex
              more powerful
              than your gods

hypocrites: do as I say
            not as I do

what

the

fuck?

I miss the kid

I never knew

I exist in shame

24

Diego

Dueñas

exists.

ashes of love and struggle

Moose | Head Shots

Thoughts of pain in my head
Targets not plain or said

It travels long like a flood
Through channels of life's blood

Night rushes in as lights go out
Frequency clears commanding attention
    all about

Spirited music moves seemingly to depths
    unknown
Imagination creates illusions mixing
    emotions as shown

Scenes like these intensify love and hate
Bringing all your secrets out as on a
    plate

Sadness or revenge in your eyes await
Time is near to dismiss or initiate.

Kenneth Andrus | Sometimes

Sometimes I can't hear myself think.
Isn't that wonderful?

ashes of love and struggle

Kenneth Andrus | Regrets

My only regrets are your last words to me.
No, my only regret is why you said
your last words to me.

RUIN | In Utero

My ego is a mirror,
Reflecting back my past.
Can you see what I mean?

My memories are my past,
And my now is my past.
Shaken or stirred?

My memories precede me,
So I cognate all stimuli rapidly.
Have you worn my socks?

My senses reach outward,
Deeply rooted in my brain.
Do you ever sleep in your dreams?
What have you grown in the dark?

I have to remember,
Or else I cannot know.
Who stole the cookies?

I intuit microscopic tsunamis
Cascading along my fibre.
Do we need to go for groceries?

I have reached inside of me,
With the other side of my mirror.
Are we there yet?

I think the world is flat,
Like a beer left open all night.
Diamonds: are they really forever?

ashes of love and struggle

My feelings correspond with each other,
Like prisoners in different countries.
What's a falling star?

My ego is my mirror.
It reposes horizonvertically,
omnispherical.

Can you deliver me in utero?

RUIN | Enter Inter - Inner

Waiting in the cold,
Waiting for the waterdoor,
the crows are watching,
and against the former.

Wait again the old,
Wade in forth war,
thick-row swatching,
and angst reformer.

Weight sagging to hold,
Way in for toward,
the craw searching,
antiglass transformer.

Whey ate saying to hole,
Wane fortward,
thick raw sea urchin,
ant eggless strains farmer.

We eight sagging told,
We hate fourth-hard,
the cross your chin,
an eagle trains far more.

Sun-arc hypotenuse,
meaning less to some,
minutes bent circular,
minus less to sum.

Burn me down now,
schizaffiendic hallelujah,
bury me below the snow.
Burgeoning, I glow.

ashes of love and struggle
RUIN | Grapefruit Vomit

Taste The Touch
    fucked was I formed of ephemeral

Waste a past
    cystemal paste of cerebral

Took too long
    and it's gone you weren't listenal

Many not knowingly
    snowing rain frozen formerly

Above a cascade
    swift rising soulcore defecate

Ciclicle depth assault
    ripely plucked out the fruited fault

Knackerman's mallet worn
    sickle icecycle of a cynical mind

Sick 'n' tired
    and fed up with a brain grind

Ship-shaped withering
    writing red razors sliding slitherly

Writhing raison d'être
    post haste poesy prayer rosary

Liquid aerodungeon
    inquisitive prying sobriety knowsilly

Suffocated rage coupon
    subliminal festival fetal bestial
    fatality

Time's gluts despotic
    carnal honor to the Necrotic Carousel

Time's glut horrorful
    captive slaves of this Cosmic
    Carnival

Infected obsidian fortitude
    inglorious ignominious ingenuously
    igneous

Photosynthesis mammalian
    worms rooted inverted foliagely
    in - vertebrated

Pleasure's driven wild
    screaming until every last shadow's
    defiled

Fallen censure ridden
    by forgotten unforgiven hungers for
    ever forbidden

Pyroclastic cataclysm
    volcanic spasm manic tectonic
    premonition

Flutter panic plethora
    cornea camera rusted memory shutter

ashes of love and struggle

Cluster colostomy floods
    inner enigma enemy enters life's
    enema

Blank backed panorama
    can't chop desolation weighed to
    waste

Formed of ephemeral
    while fucking I Touch The Taste!

Moose | You'll See Them Again

Time will tell, when all has stopped.
It will be heavenly as a cold day in hell.

Late in the day, at around brunch,
The cows will come, standing out to swim
from sharks.

Flying high, deep underground, where the
wetness of the water is driest.
You will see them again, when nothing is
out.

You call, screaming loudly, as quiet as
you can. Never, most definitely, you'll
see them again.

Never ever tell this secret that
everybody knows - or you will be cursed
with all that you could ever ask for.
Really, it blows.

Stopping only before you start
Like beginning your sentence at the end
and erasing all you will never do.

Ever completing your formless body
Rotting, fully wasted
Good as new.

Your tongue tastes, as a balloon
Bloated, as fresh grain
You'll see them again.

Jai | The Bee

As I sat solemnly, he entered the room.
Flying about, the little bee zoomed.
The door was open, so I paid him no mind.
Bees find my company from time to time.

But this unassuming bee started bothering
    me.
He landed on my shoulder and I'm allergic,
    you see?
A sting from this creature could be too
    much to bear.
He could take my very life if not handled
    with care.

So in gentle regards, I gave him a nudge.
Just a wave toward the door, for I held no
    grudge!
Toward my aim, the stranger took flight.
Relief became me at this glorious sight.

But suddenly, the bee began to dive.
The wounded warrior won't return to his
    hive?

I rose to see that little bee
Crawling about with a missing wing.
Perhaps my nudge was a bit too brace
Or maybe my shoulder was his resting
    place?

Oh well, he's fine! I watched him lurk
I sat again and returned to work

Later this day I decided to clean.
A sweep and mop in the spirit of
       Spring.
As I worked toward the door and onto the
       rug
There began to form a colony of bugs.

At this sight I was taken aback.
It appeared the insects were sharing a
       snack
And to my despair, you can imagine what I
       seen.
A struggling bee with only one wing.

In that moment, grief filled my heart
For this harmless being my hands tore
       apart.
My hasty decision was his murdering knife.
My reckless indifference had cost a life.

And call me selfish, but before me
       appeared
My own life struggles in this little bee's
       fears.

As they preyed on his downfall & prevented
       his flight
He struggled to stand with all his might.
Enemies surrounded and darkness ensued,
And the weight of his burden ensured he
       would lose.

Was his family near? Did they witness my
       crimes?
Would his absence go noticed by those
       loved & despised?

ashes of love and struggle

Empathy conjures a new point a view,
And for the first time in a long time I
    can feel what is true

Because in this being lived a spirt like
    me,
I have vowed to never harm another bee.

A Queer Prisoner's Poetry Anthology, Vol. 2

Part 3

*hurry the dream
is almost over*

RUIN | Day 10

           My original motivation becomes
obscure
     as my curiosity burgeons with the
appeal of stealing a glance
beyond
     the curtain of my own mortality
     without regard for the fleshly vessel
that transports my
self
     towards an inevitable precipice
          I can't tear away my eye from
the scene
          despite the horrific implication
of impending oblivion
          solely for the magnificent glory
     not of the coming
season
rather for the clarity with which I see
its immanent approach
     yet but not wholly
          only distinct through the almost
consciously imperceptible
     shifting in the shades and hues of
conceptual reality
     within the center of this
being
     separate from the material
ever-shriveling around this
body
     in disgusted rebellion against the
nature of fragility implicit in
life

ashes of love and struggle
    as the glint of infinite creativity
beckons
     through the apparent impasse between

dissolution and solitude

      invading my imagination
      itching my id.

Moose | Alone I Wait

I feel I've missed the one destined for
me, yet every night my mind sets you free.

Through the mist and the steam I see you
there in my dream - with all these lovers.

You are crying desperately to meet their
needs.

Surrounded by unhappiness which lingers
and hovers.

Then I see you again, in a bed hiding
under covers.

The dream seems to deepen and you fall
asleep.

Finally at peace.

Wishing that of your love you could teach.

I see you now walking the beach.

As you pass, I wave to you, but you don't
see me.

I fight my dream to allow you to stop and
look at me, yet there you go walking by.

I wish you knew where to find me.

I wish you knew that I am alive.

ashes of love and struggle

I know if I had half a chance to get you
to see me, just half a glance -

I believe you need me. Even in our dreams,
you could dance with me.

But the illusion fades.

Reality fights to invade.

Sven in this I wouldn't like to have
stayed.

Until the dream-world takes me again.

As I lie awake, I know I cannot stop until
you're here with me.

And as they say, "time will tell."

Until then my love, I wait.

Lamont K. H., Jr. | Lonely Man Doing Time

Doing time behind enemy lines can be
stressful and lonely.

Constantly asking myself: "where's all the
women, family members and fake homies."

Out of sight and out of mind when you have
a certain amount of time.

People always saying they going do this
and that but always lying.

My level of trust is at an all time low,
which makes it hard to build relationships
with people I don't know.

Sometimes I'd rather be lonely because
it's a waste of time dealing with people
who's phony.

The street life and prison left me with a
heavy heart. Thinking to myself: "Will I
continue elevating towards the light and
escape the dark?"

Loneliness, pain, disappointment and
disloyalty can damage you mentally and
spiritually - to the point that you start
looking at everyone as a potential enemy.

The truth is I just want to be loved, but
seem like don't nobody understand me.

RUIN | Hungerstrike

There is no light
>Within this darkness
>Only I can find my candle
>As the tide begins to recede
>Once strong
>Ebbing slowly away

From.....life
>Dripping dawn
>To dusk we wither

From.........life
>Completely powerless
>Over the creation
>In our own existence

From..............life
>Abounding decrepitude
>Creeps through all
>Of everything
>Near and far
>Resounds the cacophony
>Of fog and snowflakes
>Within my growing dizziness

From....................life
>While these flurries of spots
>Trace long fingers
>Down my consciousness
>As life grows cold

From.............................

L. Knight | Outreach

I stand before you, in shackles and chains
You can't see them
and they don't chafe my skin
But they bind my soul and exploit my pains
I could show you my world,
but I would never let you in.

How can I tell my story?
When is a crime not a crime?
These are questions we ask ourselves
and each other
Over and over again
while we spend our lives doing time

Start with my victims:
My Heidi,
My Father,
My Mother?

But the list too long
and many I do not know

So how do I tell my story?
How do I keep you off my path?

Your life is your road,
I can't scare you from going too fast
You decide if you drive straight,
I am but a sign of where not to go.

RUIN | Time Scavenger

Time scavenger
polychronic glutton
demonic temporal vulture

Flying through time
licking rime off a
hagfish second's spine

as days and nights revolve in flights
the sights of lights
beats
pulses

chronologically
eternity only considered repeated
infinities neurologically

psychologically incessant multitudinous

buzzing of the threshing

of seconds
minutes
hours
millennia

intermeshing

slipshod shady comprehensions
of an anthropoid's moment

losing touch with the background
of an asteroid's movement

feeling pleasure and pain split

schismatically from immortality
by screaming
bloody
birth born slaved to temporality

misery bent
inseparable into
humanity's genetic chronicles
disexistent
insufferable
life

seen through dirty cyclops monocles

we're chained woven welded to
the next
occurrence

in chairs moving seated far from rest or
reassurance

to do or be begs only for how well one's
mind stays well-filed

    while beaten to death

with the liquid nitrogen frozen carcass of

    your inner child
    breastfed biohazard waste

from the hospital incinerator's slop
bucket

ashes of love and struggle

not even Death itself abides independent
of my ability to fuck it

using the tweezers of my mind painfully
inadequately

to count each grain of sand collected from
the stone of inactivity

underneath insurmountable skies, falling
edgewise into depravity

slowly languishing in ashes of love and
struggle for

what burn on purpose within clocks arising
from chaos to depart

extinguished by the inconceivable
emptiness of eventual

perpetual deformation change coronation
solar

ages beyond universal momentum

temporary

young cosmos proceed past astronomical
cemeteries of

ancient heavenly bodies corroding
dethroned and boneless

fullness formless taken broken towards the
center of never

meaning lands for the winter on a barren
branch of a mocking tree

grown from the seed of the ephemeral
menagerie of humanity

immutable seasonless dusk absent sound

hurry the dream is almost over

quickly reality condenses transitorily

only to rain into the deserts of forever

inconsequentially evaporating through my
mind

as I glide hungrily
dipping into doomed puddles
to drink til drunk the now

I find pieces where I can
to fill canyons of cravings

surfeited consequence for
my impertinent impermanence

slime of deconstructed consciousness
life dissected into alphabetic grime
intellectual existentially incestual
bloodline

I am become, truly,
a scavenger of time.

Scary Movie | Don't You Ever Get Tired

Don't you ever get tired
Of cutting yourself on me
Trying to put back the pieces
And hoping in your belief

That your heart will be the glue
The only thing you need
That will put me back together
Into the man I used to be

Don't you ever get tired
Of biting back your screams
In your ceaseless efforts
To patch me, piece by piece

And the tears can't stop falling
Rolling gently down your cheeks
Trying to understand why
Nothing can get through to me

So before you start to speak
I beg and plead - "listen, please"
I need to get this off my chest
Hoping that I might ease

Not only the raging storm
Roiling inside of me
But also reassurance
For a heart trying desperately

To use a selfless bandaid
To plug a dam that leaks
With a strength and persistence
Majestic in its beauty
52

It hurts when I look at you
And see the pain buried deep
The scars just below the surface
And it's all because of me

I know that I am broken
Maybe beyond what you can see
To you it might sound hopeless
Probably a bit extreme

But you're looking with your heart
And not really seeing me.

Kenneth Andrus | Parole and Love

In a few months, he will be gone.
I swear, every song on the radio
will be a love song.
He broke my heart with a word.
September -
my own Heartbreak Anniversary.
My heart hurts, selfishly.
As if he wasn't going to be home soon.
As if he wasn't moving on from this
dreadful place.
As if he wasn't moving on from me.
Why wouldn't he?
How long will we be separated, him and me?
He'll have the world
and I'll just be a memory.
He was already trying to send back
the thing I gave him.
Sure, logically, I understand.
His dad doesn't know - can't know.
But still, I am a romantic at heart
with a pessimistic brain.
Now what am I supposed to do?
What are we supposed to do?
Do we hold on?
Make it work?
Will it?
Oh, God, my heart -
But I'm strong
Fuck, I'm strong!
I can do this, dammit
I will do this
I will not fold,
concede, surrender, yield
Fuck no! Not me.

RUIN | Satori

OM

                                    INSIDE

THE CUBE

                                    NO DOOR

TOUCHING

                                    TWELVE SIDES

INFINITE

                                    ALL-WINDOW

PURE SCENT

                                    UNLIGHT

NONDARK

                                    ONE TASTE

FRUITFUL

                                    INCONCEIVABLE

EMPTINESS

                                    HUM

ashes of love and struggle

Chris Lafamilia | Level Up

You witnessing a master
here at work
I ain't pro tools

Soon as you lit them
haters test your heart
like it's night school

I mark 'em no drive
call that garage,
car fume

they still see I'm cereal
this time no milk
no spoon

they know I'm here to stay
reserve hotel
all rooms

and stay away from 12
catch me 2 min
past noon

Let your guard
down they'll clean you out
like prunes do

And leave you
hanging bare
like koalas and Bamboo

You do what you
can do

No break
This ain't
Cancun

You hot, then you flop
the desert, you like
sand dunes

Just keep your head clear
invest heavy in
shampoo

Like mall food courts
martinis is a
sample

I lead by
example

Y'all just listen for details

Most people speaking lies
blowing smoke like chemtrails

No exhale
I been making calls like Nextel

While niggas steady
talking just for show
like Montel

I could never do that
I not a saint but who dat?

Move back
Swear his posture too tact

ashes of love and struggle

He rat
Relax
That's a given

My pops never raised no punk,
My mom was brilliant

Granny taught resilience
It's clear I'm worth some millions

I'm on a different scale and I've never
been reptillian

Sit back
Play my position

Let 'em wonder from a distance

Them facts speaking loud
Yet that fiction gone whisper.

Scary Movie | Living In the Moment

It doesn't matter how thick the scars get
Or how numb you get in heart and mind
It may not seem like it right now
But your aches and pain will heal in time

There is a light in the darkness
You just have to let yourself see
Beyond the tears blurring your vision
Falling down your face shamelessly

And those screams you use in rage
Filled with your despair, guilt, and pain
Thinking that no one can hear the strain
And the forlorn need to escape

There are people who are listening
Unassumingly sympathetic
Who will tell you, believe it our not
That you're loved and that you're worth it

Your suffering, your please, your grief
Your loneliness and withdrawn spirit
Your torment, distress, and anguish
And all that this world inflicts

It doesn't mean the end of your life
Nor should it be the end of your life
Although it seems unbearable
There's a spark in you to survive

Never let go of what is precious
And uniquely valuable
You are the only one of you
Pricelessly incomparable

ashes of love and struggle

I guess what I'm trying to say
Is that you're not invisible
You are not the only one to feel
As if you're alone in this world

We've all had to take it step by step
Struggling to live in the moment
Just take your time and relish each breath
And cherish life's beautiful elegance.

John & Krysta Cox | My Name

My name is that which cannot be spoken

My name is the taste upon your lips
as you kiss me

My name is the shudder that runs
through our bodies as we touch

My name is the inspiration that
takes flight as you think of me

My name is the fire of my eyes
as I look upon your courage

My name is the tenderness in my eyes
as I gaze upon your forgiveness

My name is the joy in our hearts
as they beat as one

My name is yours.

ashes of love and struggle
Willie Cleveland | Resilient

In a place so dark

We found the light

Where sad songs are sung

We found delight

Where tears are shed

We dared to laugh

Where there was no way

We found the path

Where all things lacked

We were sustained

Because what wasn't

We became.

ashes of love and struggle

Afterword

This anthology sure took the space and time it needed to grow before I knew it was ready to be released to the world. The process of editing this second collection of poetic works from the A.B.O. Comix family mirrored that of so many of the poets featured in its pages; that is to say, there was plenty of time spent in deep reflection, punctuated with brief bursts of inspiration that resulted in what you've just finished reading.

Thank you to Cass and Casper for the extra ounce of editorial and logistical help that ensured this anthology saw the light of day. And the very deepest of gratitude to all the seasoned poets and first-timers (and everyone in between) who contributed work this time around. Through your verses, y'all taught me so much about self-trust, creative responses to injustice, pulling oneself back from oblivion, and more and more. Thank you.

Please share this little book with your friends, enemies, lovers, and communities, I'm sure after making it to the end you can tell that these poems simply beg to be read. And please join me in uplifting Ms Jazzie Ferrari, David Snyder, Shyra Bryant and RUIN for inspiring the section titles, back cover text and the title of the anthology. I am lucky to share in the fruits of their love and struggle. And finally, if you're reading this from prison and you'd like to submit to our next edition, get in touch:

> A.B.O. Comix c/o Poetry Anthology
> P.O. Box 11584
> 195 41st St
> Oakland, CA 94611

- Ollie Mills

How to Help

Thank for reading this collection of poems by incarcerated queer and trans writers. We hope they have inspired you to take action on behalf of these poets to work towards a kinder, more compassionate world.

If you believe in our mission, you can help support us by:

Donating or providing resources:
paypal.me/abocomix | Venmo @abocomix
patreon.com/abocomix

Spreading the word and following us for updates:
Twitter: @AboComix
Instagram: @a.b.o.comix
Facebook: ABO Comix

Volunteering with us or hosting a fundraising event: email abocomix@gmail.com if interested!

Writing to someone on the inside: Check out www.abocomix.com/bios to get connected!

Talking to friends, family, neighbors, and community members. Open up a dialogue and remember to meet people where they're at. Don't be afraid of difficult conversations and do your best to maintain an open mind. You may learn something as well. When we know better, we can do better.

Starting your own creative project! Against all odds, we're still here. Still creating, still building friendships, still optimistic about what we can achieve when we work together. Take a chance, work hard and you will do amazing things. Trust us, we've been there.

Love and solidarity always!

www.ingramcontent.com/pod-product-compliance
Lightning Source LLC
Chambersburg PA
CBHW061323120626
46546CB00007B/2650